Wild & Wacky Pet Jokes & Riddles

Michael J. Pellowski
Illustrated by Jackie Snider

Sterling Publishing Co., Inc.
New York

To Cricket, Brandy, Bingo, Coal, Kitty, and Big Spike

Library of Congress Cataloging-in-Publication Data

Pellowski, Michael.
  Wild & wacky pet jokes & riddles / Michael J. Pellowski ; illustrated by Jackie
Snider.
      p. cm.
  Includes index.
  ISBN 1-4027-2431-4
  1. Pets--Juvenile humor. 2. Riddles, Juvenile. I. Title: Wild and wacky pet
jokes and riddles. II. Snider, Jackie. III. Title.

PN6231.P42P45 2006
818'.5402--dc22

2005023461

10 9 8 7 6 5 4 3 2 1

Published by Sterling Publishing Co., Inc.
387 Park Avenue South, New York, NY 10016
© 2006 by Michael Pellowski
Distributed in Canada by Sterling Publishing
C/o Canadian Manda Group, 165 Dufferin Street
Toronto, Ontario, Canada M6K 3H6
Distributed in the United Kingdom by GMC Distribution Services
Castle Place, 166 High Street, Lewes, East Sussex, England BN7 1XU
Distributed in Australia by Capricorn Link (Australia) Pty. Ltd.
P.O. Box 704, Windsor, NSW 2756, Australia

Sterling ISBN-13: 978-1-4027-2431-2
      ISBN-10 1-4027-2431-4

For information about custom editions, special sales, premium and
corporate purchases, please contact Sterling Special Sales
Department at 800-805-5489 or specialsales@sterlingpub.com.

CONTENTS

That's Doggone Funny!

What did one marine K-9 say to the other marine
K-9?

"*Semper Fi-Do.*"

Knock-knock!
Who's there?
Schnauzer.
Schnauzer who?
Schnauzer time for all good men to come
to the aid of their country.

What does a dog cheerleader hold in its paws?
Pom-Pomeranians.

King Midas' dog is a Golden Retriever.

BOY: We're so rich, my dog uses a gold shovel when he buries a bone.

GIRL: Well, we're so rich, my dog also uses a gold shovel when he buries a bone, but he has his butler dig the hole.

Then there was the conceited dog who was too proud to beg.

Who corrects test papers at the dog obedience school?
The Grade Dane.

What did one sled dog say to the other?
"I have more pull on this job than you do."

Which dog hosts the TV game show *Poochie's Price Is Right?*
Bob Bark-er.

POODLE: Arf! Arf! Woof! Woof! Bark! Bark!
BOY: Wow! Your Poodle is one smart dog.
GIRL: What makes you say that?
BOY: She speaks three languages fluently.

What is the theme song of Mr. President Poochie?
"Heel to the Chief."

What did the angry dog say to the pesky flea?
"Get off my back, will ya!"

What did the dog trainer say after he gave the Whippet a command?
"Get crackin', Doggie."

> Knock-knock!
> *Who's there?*
> Dew.
> *Dew who?*
> Dew not tease the dog.

MARTY: Does your dog come when you whistle?
MEL: Nope.
MARTY: Why not? Is he a bad dog?
MEL: No. I can't whistle.

What did the lunar astronaut name his dog?
Moon Rover.

What's the worst thing a dog can do on a computer?
Go to FleaBay.

Show me a smart Border Terrier...and I'll show you a dog who knows its own boundaries.

What did one police dog say to the other?
"Let's follow that cur."

CRAZY CALLING CARDS

Mr. I. M. A. Baldy—Breeder of hairless dogs.

Mr. Garr Lick—Trainer of Italian Greyhounds.

Mr. A. B. Type—Breeder of Bloodhounds.

Mr. Mega Bucks—Breeder of prize Deerhounds.

Mr. Al Cook—Breeder of Chow Chows.

What dance did the French Poodle teach the Chihuahua?
  The Mexican-can.

  Knock-knock!
    Who's there?
  Otto.
    Otto who?
  Otto want a cat. I want a pet dog.

CRAZY QUESTION

Do watchdogs ever suffer from tick infestation?

MATT: My pet dog is a Boxer.
PAT: Big deal! My Japanese Spaniel is a martial arts expert.

Which dog was a great public speaker?
  Spaniel Webster.

OBSERVATION

Sigmund Freud's Poodle spends too much time on the psychiatrist's couch.

Which pet pooch sings rap songs?
  Snoop-Doggie.

DAFFY DEFINITION

Vet—a dog healer.

☆ OBSERVATION

Well-trained dog actors know how to give a command performance.

My dog is such a good actor, he got a part in a Broadway murder mystery—playing dead.

> Knock-knock!
>> *Who's there?*
> S. Mel.
>> *S. Mel who?*
> S. Mel buried bones. Let's start digging.

My purebred dog...
is so well trained, she won't sit down unless you pull out a chair for her.

VINNIE: My dog won't do any tricks unless you feed him his supper first.
MINNIE: Oh, your dog is an after-dinner speaker.

GIRL: That's a funny-looking police dog.
BOY: He's a copper spaniel.

What does a Dachshund use to play golf?
A very, very short kennel club.

BOWSER: I got a part in the obedience school production of *Oliver Twist*.
FIDO: What role do you play?
BOWSER: I'm the Arf-ful Dodger.

Knock-knock!
  Who's there?
Harriet.
  Harriet who?
Harriet up or she'll make us late for Poochie's party.

CRAZY QUESTION

Do Alaskan sled dogs watch Mush-see TV?

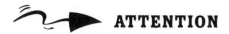 **ATTENTION**

In the K-9 Corps the officers bark orders.

Police dogs like to collar cat burglars.

What was Captain Kirk's dog on *Star Trek*?
  Mr. Spot.

What does an Italian Greyhound like to fetch?
  A spicy meatball.

Which dog is really cute?
  The Foxhound.

What kind of pet does Dracula have?
  A Bloodhound.

What is a pooch's favorite football team?
  The Green Bay Dog Packers.

GIRL: Does your watchdog speak?
BOY: No. But he tocks a lot.

PATIENT: Please help me, Doc. When I look at my
  dog I see spots before my eyes.
DOCTOR: Relax. Your dog is a Dalmatian.

FUN FACT

I know a baseball pitcher who is such a control
freak he refuses to walk his own dog.

YOU TELL 'EM, POOCHIE

You tell 'em, Scotch Terrier...it's a kilter joke.

You tell 'em, Doggie...heel listen to you.

You tell 'em, Sleeping Dog...and don't lie.

You tell 'em, Muttsy...it's a flea country.

You tell 'em, Watchdog...and take your time.

You tell 'em, Pug...this story is a real knockout.

You tell 'em, Hunting Dog...and don't cry woof.

You tell 'em, Pit Bull...it's a sic story.

You tell 'em, Bowser...they're barking up your
family dogwood tree.

VET: So, what's the problem with your dog?

CLIENT: I tied him to a ten-foot rope, and he broke it. When he came back, I tied him to the remaining seven feet of rope, and he broke it. After he came back again I tied him to the last five feet of rope, and he broke it. You've got to help me, Doc, I'm at the end of my rope.

How do a pack of happy dogs travel across the country?

They form a tail-waggin' train.

BOY: My pet pooch is a bird dog.
GIRL: Does he like doggie tweets?

BOY: Do you think my dog is too fat?
VET: No. He's just a heavyweight Boxer.

STACY: Why is your dog twitching?
TRACY: She's a Flinch Poodle.

What kind of dog replaces old shingles?
A roof-roofer.

What kind of dog likes to play jumping games?
A Hop Scotch Terrier.

BENNY: Which breed of dog is the most athletic?
LENNY: A Jock Russell Terrier.

BOY: I have a Russian Wolfhound, a French Poodle, and a Mexican Chihuahua.
GIRL: Gee, don't any of your pets understand English

BEST-SELLING DOG BOOKS

Life in a Boarding School—by Ken L. Club

How to Train Mixed-Breed Pups— by Lotta Mutz

Teach Your Dog Tricks—by Sheik Hans Boyz

Exercise Your Pooch—by Les Gopher Awok

Which vegetable does Lassie like to eat?
Collie-flower.

SIGN IN A DOG OBEDIENCE SCHOOL

Speak only when spoken to.

WOMAN: Is my husband really as sick as a dog?
DOCTOR: Yes. Your husband has the measles.
WOMAN: Well, what do you know. I thought he was
just pretending to be a Dalmatian.

What did the dinosaur name his pet dog?
   T-Rex.

KEN: My dog is a Boxer.
BEN: Does he have a ring around his collar?

Knock-knock!
   Who's there?
Irish Terriers.
   Irish Terriers who?
Irish Terriers would magically appear
before every child who wants a dog!

Knock-knock!
   Who's there?
Willis.
   Willis who?
Willis dog ever
stop barking?

Knock-knock!
   Who's there?
Saluke.
   Saluke who?
Saluke over there and tell me
what you see.

16

Knock-knock!
Who's there?
Hugo.
Hugo who?
Hugo feed the dog right now.

Knock-knock!
Who's there?
Lassie.
Lassie who?
Lassie how much this dog collar costs.

Knock-knock!
Who's there?
Omelet.
Omelet who?
Omeletting your dog out, okay?

Knock-knock!
Who's there?
Pekingese.
Pekingese who?
Pekingese boxes and you'll know what you're getting for Christmas.

Knock-knock!
Who's there?
Egos.
Egos who?
Egos home to walk his dog at noon.

Knock-knock!
Who's there?
Whippet.
Whippet who?
Whippet until it becomes creamy frosting.

Knock-knock!
Who's there?
The Labrador.
The Labrador who?
The Labrador's open.

BOY: Why does my dog always run away?
GIRL: Maybe he's wearing a flee collar.

GIRL: Does your pet pooch do any tricks?
BOY: One, but he won't perform it now. We're not on speaking terms.

WOMAN: I love my dog so much I bought her a diamond flea collar.
MAN: That won't scare fleas away. It'll attract them.
WOMAN: What do you mean?
MAN: When the fleas see the diamonds they'll know your dog has good taste.

18

They crossed a pooch with a homing pigeon and got a dog who never gets lost.

What did Porky Pig say to his pet dog?
"Don't bite the ham that feeds you."

My dog...
is so lazy, the only way he'll go for a walk is if I carry him.

What kind of dog does Bambi have?
A Deerhound.

What kind of pet pooch does Santa Claus have?
A Husky. It's his sled dog.

Who is Santa's best sled dog?
Rudolph the Red-nosed Reindeerhound.

MATT: My dog is like a member of the family.
PAT: Now that you mention it, he does kind of
    resemble you.

My dog...
    is so smart he doesn't just speak, he recites
    poetry.

JACK: Where's the best place to buy a mixed-breed puppy?

MACK: Go to a new cur dealer.

 ## CRAZY QUESTION

When Bloodhounds have a cold, do they smell bad?

What do you call half a dozen dogs in a group?
  A six-pack of pooches.

SIGN IN A POOCH DATING SERVICE

Let us help you. After all, it's a dog-meet-dog world out there.

Which dog works for the circus?
  The sideshow barker.

We're so rich...
  my dog doesn't bury his bones. He keeps them in a wall safe.

BOY: Don't bathe your Dalmatian too often.

GIRL: Why not?

BOY: You don't want to get him spotlessly clean, do you?

MICK: My dog was in the navy.
NICK: Did he serve on a battleship?
MICK: No. He was on a pet carrier.

WACKY WANT AD

Vets needed to examine Dalmatians—spot checkers.

GIRL: Did you hear about the pooch who discovered
   a dinosaur skeleton and ran away in fear?
BOY: No. Why did he do that?
GIRL: He didn't want to meet up with the dog who
   buried that bone.

Knock-knock!
Who's there?
Stable.
Stable who?
Stable. Be a good dog, Bill, and stay.

What does a pooch use to row a canoe?
A doggie paddle.

What do you get if you cross a greyhound with a giraffe?
A canine who wins a lot of dog races by a neck.

GINA: Why is your sled dog wearing skis?
TINA: He likes to chase snowmobiles.

Why didn't the baseball pooch slide into home?
He was afraid of the dog catcher.

MEL: Your dog is pretty old.
NELL: Thank you. She was even prettier when she was young.

What do you get if you cross a cantaloupe with Lassie?
A melon-Collie dog.

IGOR: I think your dog is barking to come in. You'd better go and see.
IVAN: Sorry. I never go outside when there's a woof at my door.

BOY: My dog is so smart he won't go for a ride in the car unless we put a seat belt on him.

GIRL: Well, my dog is so smart when we go for a ride in the car, he wants to drive.

I knew...
  a rich Irish dog who was a jet-Setter.

⭐ OBSERVATION

Gardeners who plant dogwood near pussy willows may develop bark problems.

GIRL: Cats are smarter than dogs. Dogs are so dumb they can't climb trees.

BOY: My dog is smart enough to climb all the way to the top of a tree.

GIRL: So why doesn't he do it?

BOY: He's afraid of heights.

Just Kitten Around!

Which famous cat sings country mewsic songs?
  Dolly Purrton.

Who is the tallest cat ever to play pro basketball?
  Meow Ming.

Why was Meow Ming taken out of the basketball game?
  He had too many purr-sonal fouls.

Knock-knock!
Who's there?
Tabby.
Tabby who?
Tabby or not tabby, that is the question.

How do cats get into heaven?
Through the purrly gates.

CLARA: Why do cats climb trees?
SARA: Because trees don't have stairs or elevators.

What kind of cat makes a good pet for a ghost?
  A boo Persian.

What kind of cat makes a good pet for a librarian?
  A well-read tabby.

What kind of cat makes a good pet for a dairy farmer?
  A cream Persian.

What kind of cat makes a good pet for the Abominable Snowman?
  A Himalayan.

What do you get if you cross a vampire with a long-haired kitty?
  A fangora cat.

TOM CAT: I drive a Jaguar.
KITTY CAT: Big deal! I drive a Mouseratti.

What kind of cat likes meat for breakfast?
  The sausage lynx.

What do NFL cats play?
  Pussyfootball.

BOY: Your cat sounds like a clock.
GIRL: That's because she's wearing a flea and tick-
  tock collar.

BOY: My cat is a messy eater.
GIRL: Give him a catnapkin.

BOY: How do you order a kitten by mail?
GIRL: Look through a cat-a-log.

Where did Leonardo Cat Vinci display his artwork?
  In a mewseum.

GIRL: I lost my cat. Please help me find it.
POLICEMAN: You'll have to file a missing purrson
  report.

NOTICE

Cool cats like to watch mewsic videos.

What do you call a kitten who costs a penny?
  A purr-cent.

FAMOUS KITTY LIT

Tom (cat) Sawyer

Mewtiny on the Bounty

A Tale of Two Kitties

Uncle Tom's Cabin

VENDOR: What do you want on your hot dog?
CAT: Moustard.

How can you tell if your kitty is a computer cat?
If she's a computer cat, she'll like to sleep on laptops.

Why did the girl give her cat a cell phone?
To make it easier to call her kitty.

Knock-knock!
Who's there?
Annie.
Annie who?
Annie body seen my lost cat?

SILLY SIGN

On a North Pole pet shop:
We have the coolest cats in the world.

JIM: Why is your cat clawing up that mail?
TIM: It's his scratching post.

UFO researcher: I have a cat who had a close encounter of the thirst kind with a flying saucer of milk.

OSCAR: Did you ever see *Cats* on Broadway?
EMMY: No, but once I saw mice scamper down Madison Avenue.

 **WANTED**

Domestic cat needed to do light mousework.

TOM CAT: Can I talk to you man to man?
BOB CAT: No. But you can talk to me Persian to
Persian.

What did Juliecat say when she stepped out on the balcony?
"*Ro-meow, Ro-meow…*"

MR. CAT: They're building a kennel up the street.
MRS. CAT: We've got to move out of this
neighborhood before it goes to the dogs.

What is a cat's favorite color?
  Purr-ple.

Knock-knock!
  Who's there?
Manx.
  Manx who?
"Manx for the Memories!"

Knock-knock!
  Who's there?
Hairy.
  Hairy who?
Hairy home with my new kitten.

Knock-knock!
  Who's there?
A catamaran.
  A catamaran who?
A catamaran away,
but it came back later.

Knock-knock!
  Who's there?
A cathode.
  A cathode who?
A cathode a mouse in the air
and then gently caught it.

Knock-knock!
  Who's there?
I'm just a kitten.
  I'm just a kitten who?
I'm just a kitten you.
Ha ha! I'm really a dog.

Knock-knock!
  Who's there?
Mike Att.
  Mike Att who?
Mike Att purrs when
it's happy.

Knock-knock!
  Who's there?
M. T.
  M. T. who?
M. T. the litter box!

Knock-knock.
  Who's there?
I fonda.
  I fonda who?
I fonda lost kitten.

Knock-knock!
  Who's there?
Ann.
  Ann who?
Ann-Gora cats have
pretty fur.

Knock-knock!
  Who's there?
Mike Hitton.
  Mike Hitton who?
Mike Hitton is a little
Siamese cat.

Knock-knock!
  Who's there?
Pussy willow.
  Pussy willow who?
Pussy willow kitty
money if kitty gives her
a loan.

What did the cat philosopher say?
  "We live in an impurr-fect world."

Knock-knock!
  Who's there?
I'm feline.
  I'm feline who?
I'm feline fine. How are you?

Why do cats lick milk out of bowls?
  Because they don't know how to use a spoon.

MAGICIAN'S WIFE: Our cat disappeared.
MAGICIAN: Oh, no! You gave it vanishing cream instead of milk.

GIRL: My two cats are bitter enemies. What can I do?
VET: Stop giving them sour milk.

My cat...
is so finicky tuna isn't good enough for her. She wants lobster for dinner.

What does a kitty take camping?
A *cat-nap-sack*.

Then there was the cat who had a fight with a saucer of milk and got in some pretty good licks!

What do you call a kitty who has her fur done up in cornrows?
A *braidy cat*.

I know...
a doctor whose cat is a first-aid kit.

What do you call twenty cats marching down the street holding mewsical instruments?
A *purr-ade*.

BOY: I used to be my teacher's pet.
GIRL: Couldn't she afford a cat or a dog?

Knock-knock!
Who's there?
Tijuana.
Tijuana who?
Tijuana see my cat's kittens?

Knock-knock!
Who's there?
Howell.
Howell who?
Howell the cat get in if you don't open the door?

What did the cat say to the K-9 dog before he chased her?

"*Dog tag, you're it.*"

SIGN AT THE SWIM CLUB

All young cats are required to use the kitty pool.

SILLY SIGN

Gentle Kitty Groomers—we handle your cat with kit gloves.

BILL: How can you tell if a cat burglar has been in your house?

WILL: Your cat will be missing.

GIRL: Do you want to hear me call my rabbit and my cat both at the same time?

BOY: Sure.

GIRL: Okay! Hare-Kitty! Hare-Kitty! Hare-Kitty-Kitty!

What kind of lottery tickets do cats buy?
The scratch-off kind.

What do you call a feline who writes stories for a newspaper?
A copy cat.

What do you call a sloppy cat?
A mess kit.

KIT: Why do they call this event a milk marathon?

CAT: Because it takes a lot of laps to finish the race.

CRAZY QUESTIONS

Do cats ever get dog tired?

Do weary dogs take catnaps?

Do Alaskan cats use dogsleds in the winter?

MILLIE: Yesterday my cat jumped into the tub while I was bathing.

TILLIE: That's odd.

MILLIE: Not really. I was taking a milk bath.

YOU TELL 'EM

You tell 'em, Kitty...and don't stray from the topic.

You tell 'em, Tom Cat...this story is right up your alley.

You tell 'em, Manx...it's a short tale.

> Knock-knock.
> > *Who's there?*
> Icy.
> > *Icy who?*
> Icy your cat had kittens again.

Which party game do cats like to play?
> *Mewsical chairs.*

Knock-knock!
Who's there?
Norway.
Norway who?
Norway am I cleaning out the bird cage
again. It's your turn.

MR. TOUCAN: I wrote a musical play about a canary
who likes to shop.
MR. PARROT: What's it called?
MR. TOUCAN: *Buy, Buy Birdie!*

ZACK: I have a woodpecker and a crow.
MACK: That must be a lot of work.
ZACK: It is. I'm always at their peck and caw.

CHESTER: Do you like having a pet duck?
LESTER: It's not as much fun as it's quacked up to be.

BIRDIE BOOKS

Reward Your Bird with Treats—by Polly Von Acracker

Breed Little Yellow Birds—by Ken Airy

Raising Hatchlings—by Bertie Nestor

My canary...
won so many merit badges, he's now an Eagle Scout.

MARTY: Listen to that toucan. It's talking about algebra and geometry.
ARTIE: It must have been a math teacher's pet.

Knock-knock!
Who's there?
Bird A.
Bird A who?
Bird A parties are fun.

VAN: Why haven't all your homing pigeons landed yet?

DAN: Don't worry. This kind of fowl-up is not unusual.

Which bird was married to a president of the United States?

Lady Bird Johnson.

PARIS: I named my duck Hilton.

MARIS: Why?

PARIS: He has a big hotel bill.

BIRD INVENTIONS WE NEED

Cages with tape recorders for parrots who talk in their sleep and want to know what they said.

Cages with mini hot tubs instead of birdbaths.

Tiny CD players for birds to sing along with.

Birdcages with mini microphones for canaries who like to pretend they're professional singers.

My parrot...
is so spoiled she won't eat a cracker unless it has caviar on it.

JOE: Why did you let all your pigeons out?
MOE: They needed exercise. They've been cooped
   up all week.

TONY: Why do you have two talking birds?
JONI: The mynah bird is from Spain and speaks
   only Spanish. The parrot speaks Spanish and
   English. He's our translator.

Carved on a bird's tombstone: "Polygon."

What game do you play with a baby parrot?
   Peck-a-boo.

What do you get if you cross a pigeon with a
chicken?
   A coo-coo cluck.

> Knock-knock!
>   *Who's there?*
> A bird Cajun.
>   *A bird Cajun who?*
> A bird Cajun that pet store costs a lot of
> money.

Why did the corn farmer buy a parrot?
   He wanted a pet who could talk his ears off.

What's the first thing a canary does when he wants
to make an investment?
   He gets together some seed money.

CRAZY QUESTION

After a long migration, do birds need flu shots?

What did Mr. Bird say to the groom at his daughter's wedding?
  "You'd better tweet her right."

BETTY: I have a terrific pet owl.
EDDIE: What's his name?
BETTY: Owlexander the Great.

PENNY: What did you feed your duck last night?
JENNY: Quackeroni and cheese.

What do you get if you cross a parrot with a pig?
A bird that hogs the conversation.

BOY: Hey, your pet owl just said, "Who, what, where, when, and why?"
GIRL: Don't pay any attention to him. He's been watching too many crime shows on TV.

BEN: My dog used to be in the K-9 Corps.
JEN: Big deal. My bird was in the parrot troopers.

HARRY: My parrot used to belong to an English teacher.
LARRY: Is he smart enough to repeat what I say or ain't he?
HARRY: He's so smart, he'll repeat what you say and also correct your grammar.

What do you get if you cross a bird with a snake?
A feather boa.

 **NOTICE**

Mother canaries bake chocolate chirp cookies for their children.

The Reptile File

What did the lizard order at the fast food burger restaurant?

French flies.

GIRL: Do you enjoy reading about snakes?
BOY: Yes. I love to coil up with a good book at night.

KELLY: My pet chameleon is always welcome at parties.
NELLIE: Why is that?
KELLY: Because he blends right in wherever he goes.

CHAD: How many days of the week does your iguana warm himself in front of his heat lamp?
BRAD: When you're an iguana, every day is sun day.

GIRL: Do you know lizards catch flies with their tongues?
BOY: Gosh! I use a baseball mitt.

BRIAN: Does your iguana's house have an attic?
RYAN: No. But it has a crawl space.

BOY: I know that my pet boa adores me.
GIRL: How do you know that?
BOY: When I take him out of his cage, he wraps himself around my body and hugs me tight. Now that's love.
GIRL: You'd better be careful he doesn't love you to death.

Show me a gecko who climbs up a wall...and I'll show you a stuck-up pet lizard.

BOA: What kind of job do you have?
GARTER SNAKE: I'm a civil serpent.

ATTENTION

Poisonous snakes should take care never to bite their own tongue.

AGENT: There's a new comedy trio called Two Stooges and a Boa Constrictor.
REPORTER: What are their real names?
AGENT: Moe, Larry, and Coily.

What gecko can perform magic tricks?
The Lizard of Oz.

Which snake discovered the Pacific Ocean?
Balboa Constrictor.

What kind of boa constrictor lives in a citrus grove?
One that squeezes oranges and grapefruits.

Knock-knock!
Who's there?
Move tortoise.
Move tortoise who?
Move tortoise and approach very slowly.

BOY: Is that gecko on the wall for sale?
PET STORE OWNER: Yes.
BOY: What's its sticker price?

What reptile can you sometimes find in a clogged drain?
A plumber's snake.

What do you get if you cross an iguana with a baseball player?
An outfielder who eats flies.

What do you get if you cross a tortoise, wool, and a boa constrictor?
A turtleneck sweater that chokes you.

What do you call a King snake?
Hiss Majesty.

CRAZY QUESTION

Do geckos like to play stickball?

Knock-knock!
  Who's there?
Sal.
  Sal who?
Sal-Amander.

FUN FACT

A gecko went out for dinner with a turtle and the gecko got stuck with the bill.

TEACHER: Use the word "gecko" in a sentence.
STUDENT: This morning my mother said, "Gecko-ing or you'll be late for school."

What happens when a turtle loses his confidence?
  He becomes a shell of his former self.

NOTICE

Geckos are good workers because they stick to their jobs.

Which veggie do snakes like?
  Asp-aragus.

What do you get if you cross frogs with iguanas?
  Leapin' lizards.

Knock-knock!
  Who's there?
Reptile.
  Reptile who?
Reptile off the floor
before you cover the
floor with carpeting.

Knock-knock!
  Who's' there?
You tortoise.
  You tortoise who?
You tortoise a lot in
class today.

What is the toughest outfit in the lizard armed
forces?
  The Marine Iguanas.

LITTLE JOHN: Robin Hood had a pet snake.
RICHARD: How do you know that?
LITTLE JOHN: Haven't you ever heard of Robin Hood's famous long boa and arrows?

Why do reptiles make good pastry chefs?
They love to bake in the sun.

What should you give an injured baby alligator?
Gator-aid.

What did the cop say to the burglar who had stolen geckos in his hands?
"Stick 'em up!"

YOU TELL 'EM

You tell 'em, Lizard...it's a cold-blooded tale.

You tell 'em, Gecko...and stick to the facts.

You tell 'em, Alligator...and make it snappy.

You tell 'em, Snake...and don't stick your tongue out when you're done.

You tell 'em, Turtle...and don't go too fast.

You tell 'em, Boa...your tale will crush their egos.

Which event did the lizard compete in at the Olympic Games?
Gecko-Roman wrestling.

What did the vet say to the sick snake?
"I need to know your medical hiss-tory."

Who did Mr. Boa marry?
His old coilfriend. She was always his main squeeze.

Who invented the lizard phone?
Salamander Graham Bell.

Knock-knock!
Who's there?
Viper.
Viper who?
Viper face, it's filthy-dirty.

GIRL: I'd rather have a cat than a turtle.
BOY: Why?
GIRL: A cat is more fun to pet than a turtle.
BOY: I'd rather have a dog than a turtle.
GIRL: Why?
BOY: Playing fetch with a turtle takes too long.

TIM: How did you pay for your pet turtle?
JIM: I just shelled out the cash.

BOY: It must be cold outside.
GIRL: What makes you say that?
BOY: I just saw an iguana wearing a turtleneck
    sweater.

Horsing Around

75% ► Tess
12% ► Nicki
10% ► Beau
3% ► Bucky

How do you find out which horse is the most popular among riders?
Take a Gallop Poll.

Knock-knock!
Who's there?
Mare.
Mare who?
Mare E. Christmas!

DINA: Do you wear boots when you ride your horse?

TINA: No. I wear saddle shoes.

Who has four legs and charges windmills? *Donkey Ote.*

MARY: Have you ever raced against your pet pony?

JERRY: Yes, but not furlong.

JUDY: Can your horse dance?

RUDY: Yes. He's a foxtrotter.

 **WANT AD**

Busy stable needs breakfast cook to make oatmeal for hungry horses.

MAN #1: My son used to ride his pony all the time. Now he's more interested in midget cars.

MAN #2: It sounds like he's putting the go-kart before the horse.

MR. STALLION: Go out and buy me a newspaper, son.

PONY BOY: What should I use for money?

MR. STALLION: Use your horse cents.

HORSE: I'm tired of running on this track.

TRAINER: I told you to pace yourself.

FLORA: Why can't my stallion run in this horse race?

CORA: Because it's a mare-a-thon.

KEN: Is that horse a friend of Mino?

LEN: Yes. He's a Palomino.

FARMER: Did I just see you trot around a hog?

MAN: Yes. I took my horse for a ride around the pork.

What type of jewelry did Mr. Horse buy for Ms. Donkey?

He bought her a bray-celet.

Do racehorses play donkey basketball?
  No. They're track stars.

STU: Why did you name your horses Sailor and
  Swabby?
LOU: Because they're stable mates.

GROOM: I'm really depressed today.
JOCKEY: Well, get my horse ready to ride anyway.
GROOM: No. I won't saddle him with my problems.

MAN #1: Do you stand behind the pets you sell?
MAN #2: No way! I'm a horse trader.

CAL: I wrote a book called *Bronc Riding*.
HAL: I'll read it just for kicks.

WIFE: Is that a mule deer?
HUSBAND: No. It's a donkey, honey.

Knock-knock!
   Who's there?
Mayors.
   Mayors who?
Mayors eat oats and so do stallions.

Knock-knock!
   Who's there?
A bridle.
   A bridle who?
A bridle sometimes cry on her
wedding day.

Why did the little horse go to the carnival?
   He wanted to go on the pony rides.

What does a horse wear in the summer?
   Jockey shorts.

Knock-knock!
   Who's there?
Mule.
   Mule who?
Mule be sorry if you adopt a pony instead
of a donkey.

DAFFY DEFINITION

Racehorse—a barn athlete.

EDDIE: I have a quarter horse for a pet.
TEDDY: Gee, I thought a horse would cost more than that.

SCIENTIST: I crossed a pony with a duck.
VET: Horse feathers!

PAUL: My pet horses are named Ringo, John, and George.
JUDE: What do Ringo, John, and George eat, Paul?
PAUL: Hay, Jude.

MAN: When your pet colt grows up are you going to race him?
BOY: Are you kidding? He already runs faster than I do.

⭐ PUN FUN

JUDY: I'm sure a Morgan horse is a light horse.
RUDY: What gave you that bright idea?

JUDY: I'm telling you, a thoroughbred can go up to forty miles per hour.
RUDY: Oh, stop running off at the mouth.

JUDY: An Arabian horse is a desert breed.
RUDY: Oh, dry up about horses already.

JACK: I ride my stallion in the morning. I ride my pony in the afternoon.
JILL: What do you ride in the evening?
JACK: My nightmare.

> Knock-knock!
> *Who's there?*
> An apple.
> *An apple who?*
> An apple-loosa is a spotted horse.

Bugged

WILL: That's your pet, that big, ugly, hairy, scary tarantula?

JILL: Yes. Isn't he adorable?

GIRL: What does your pet lizard eat?

BOY: Bugs.

GIRL: Remind me never to bring my pets over to play with your lizard.

BOY: Why not?

GIRL: I have an ant farm.

What trick did the spider perform on its motorcycle?

A spinning wheelie.

BOY: My pet spider is very nervous.
GIRL: Is he afraid of strangers?
BOY: Yes. They drive him up the wall.

What kind of music do you play for an ant farm? .

The Beatles.

What did Mr. Spider say to Ms. Firefly?

"You glow, girl!"

MOTHER: Did you spend the entire day on your computer?
BOY: Yes. I made a Web page for my pet tarantula.

What did the spider say to the homeowner?

"Can I live with you? I need a place to weave my stuff."

Knock-knock!
Who's there?
Tara-Ann.
Tara-Ann who?
Tara-Ann-Tulas are big spiders.

Knock-knock!
Who's there?
Webby.
Webby who?
Webby back in time to take care of our pet tarantula.

ANT #1: I hate suppertime.
ANT #2: Why?
ANT #1: Every night it's the same crumby food.

YOU TELL 'EM

You tell 'em, Ant...and don't stop until they cry uncle.

You tell 'em, Spider...you spin a good tale.

You tell 'em, Ant...and don't step out of line.

BOY: I have a pony and an ant farm.
GIRL: Oh! You're a horse-and-buggy kind of guy.

GIRL: My three cats are such fussy eaters. Last night I had to feed each one something different. One had chicken. One had fish. And one had liver.
BOY: Thank heaven I never have that problem with my pets.
GIRL: Why?
BOY: Because I have an ant farm.

SARA: How do you keep your ant farm germ-free?
CLARA: I use special ant-iseptic spray.

Why is an ant farm a healthy thing to have?
It's full of antibodies.

MAN: My pet store only sells ant farms and rabbits.
WOMAN: What do you call your shop?
MAN: The Bugs Bunny Store.

BOY: Do those insects own their own ant farm?
GIRL: No. They're ten-ant farmers.

GIRL: Do you ever take your ant farm out for a
   walk in the summer?
BOY: No. But sometimes I take them on a picnic.

What do you get if you cross a pet spider with a
   pet hare?
A pet webbit.

Are pet bugs afraid of policemen?
Only if they're members of a SWAT team.

Jump for Joy

What rabbit hands out parking tickets?
Meter Cottontail.

Knock-knock!
Who's there?
Rabbit.
Rabbit who?
Rabbit on a racehorse and lost. Boo-hoo!

OLLIE: Was Bambi's mother a rabbit?
DOLLIE: No, silly. You can't get deer from hare.

SIGN ON A PET STORE

Stop in for our Leap Year Frog Sale.

My pet toad...
   joined the navy. Now's he's a frogman.

JILL: I have a new pet frog.
BILL: You already toad me that.
JILL: Well, I also have a new pet rabbit.
BILL: I don't want to hare about it.

Which rabbit makes dress suits for men?
   Peter Cottontailor.

DON: My pet rabbit works in a hotel part time.
RON: What does he do?
DON: He's a bellhop.

What do you get if you cross a rabbit's ears with a computer?
   Floppy discs.

Which rabbit is a sorcerer?
   Hare E. Potter.

What's yellow and hops?
   A blond hare.

How do you get a lazy rabbit to begin a race?
   Jump-start it.

 **CRAZY QUESTIONS**

Do rabbit rappers really love hip-hop music?

Do rabbits keep in shape by doing jumping jacks?

Do kangaroos read pocketbooks?

ELMO: Dogs are lazier than rabbits.
EDNA: What makes you say that?
ELMO: In the morning my dog just rolls over, but my rabbit hops right out of bed.

MACK: Why is there a rabbit on your head?
ZACK: Because it's hunting season.
MACK: So what?
ZACK: No one would dare harm a hare on my head.

CLIENT: Please help me, Doc. My pet rabbit escaped from his pen around 5 A.M.
VET: What a shame! Another case of early hare loss.

Which rabbit was the thirty-third president of the United States?
Hare E. Truman.

MICK: Is it difficult to take care of a pet kangaroo?
RICK: The job keeps me hopping.

What do you get if you cross a rabbit with an Irish Setter?
A hare setter.

What did the rabbit running for president say to the frog and the kangaroo?

"Hop on my bandwagon."

MARLA: My pet rabbit can't jump. There's something wrong with him.

DARLA: Take him to a pet hops-pital.

What goes hop, hop hop! Ouch?

A pet kangaroo in a room with a low ceiling.

What do you have if your pet rabbit keeps tripping?

You have a problem with falling hare.

YOU TELL 'EM

You tell 'em, Toad...they won't jump
down your throat.

You tell 'em, Rabbit...and don't jump
to any conclusions.

You tell 'em, Kangaroo...you're hopping
mad.

You tell 'em, Froggie...they'll flip out
when they hear your story.

KELLY: You can't use that to comb your cat's fur.
SHELLY: Why not?
KELLY: It's a hare brush.

What does a rabbit put in its coffee?
Hare cream.

MARY: Do you want to hear a cute story about my
pet rabbit?
JERRY: No. I'm sick of cotton tales.

Who do you get if you cross a baby chick with a
rabbit?
Peeper Cottontail.

Funny Furry Friends

Who teaches baby guinea pigs to gnaw on things?
The chew-chew trainer.

How does a guinea pig get up to the second floor of his cage?
He uses the ham-stairs.

What do you get if you cross a hamster with a frog?
A hamphibian.

JOE: Does your pet white rat like to eat cheesecake?
MOE: No. He's a pie rat.

Which little pet played on the Women's U.S. Olympic soccer team?
Mia Hamster.

GIRL: These are my three hamsters. This one is Ham Solo and that one is Obie-Ham Kenobi.
BOY: What's the name of the one nibbling on that stick?
GIRL: Oh! That's Chewbarka.

I just gave my two pet mice a bath. Now they're both squeaky clean.

DANNY: That must be a rich pet ferret.
ANNIE: What makes you say that?
DANNY: She has a mink coat.

Who does a mouse pitcher throw his ball to?
The rat catcher.

Who invented the rodent airplane?
Wilbur and Orville Wright Mice.

What do small rodents drink instead of coffee?
Mice tea.

MR. RAT: What are we having for dinner?
MRS. RAT: Cheese steaks and mice-a-roni.

MOLLY: Would you like a sheep for a pet?
LOLLY: I shear would.

What does a pet computer mouse wear?
  A high-tech collar.

Where can you buy a pet computer mouse?
  Try eekBay.

Where does a country computer mouse live?
  With the farmer in the Dell computer.

What did the computer mouse do when his master brought home a pet duck?

He downloaded it and made it a disc-o-duck.

BOY: Have you ever seen a hamster?
GIRL: No. But once a pig glared at me for a long time.

What did Mr. Hamster say to Ms. Hamster while they were on the exercise wheel?

"We've been going around together for a long time. Let's get engaged."

PAM: My little pet goat is very naughty.
SAM: Don't be mad. He's really not such a bad kid.

Where does a hamster keep his money?
In a guinea piggy bank.

Which furry pet was the sixteenth president of the United States?
Abrahamster Lincoln.

What rodent plays shortstop on the pet baseball team?
The infield mouse.

What does a mouse use to play golf?
Mickey Mouse Clubs.

KIM: How did the teacher find out you brought your guinea pig to school today?
JIM: My own pet squealed on me.

What is a hamster's favorite TV show?
The Exercise Wheel of Fortune.

What sheep was a great baseball centerfielder?
Woolly Mays.

Fishy Tales

What does a goldfish use when it wants to borrow a book?

A library cod.

GIRL: My pet fish is sick. What should I do?
BOY: Take him to a marine vet.

PET STORE OWNER: Would you like me to give you some free pet fish?
BOY: I would, but no tanks.

Where do you keep a professional pet fish?
In a goldfish pro bowl.

CRAZY QUESTION

Do baby fish mind having wet diapers?

CHESTER: I'm training my goldfish to compete in a
marathon.
LESTER: How are you doing that?
CHESTER: Every morning I put some running water
in his fishbowl.

YOU TELL 'EM

You tell 'em, Sea Horse...and don't be
crabby.

You tell 'em, Sea Horse...and don't use any
salty language.

You tell 'em, Fishy...and don't make me worm
the story out of you.

JACK: My parents bought me a snail for a pet.
JILL: How do you feel about that?
JACK: I slowly grew to like it.

What do you get if you cross a fish with a soldier?
An aquamarine.

BOY: Will you bless the pets in my fishpond?
MINISTER: Okay. But I'm not much of a pool prayer.

What's a high-tech goldfish?
It's one that has digital scales.

A little girl looked in the fish tank in the pet store and then went up to the owner.

"Excuse me," said the girl. "Why does that one fish always swim at the rear of the school?"

"That fish," said the pet store owner, "is the back perch."

What patriotic song do fish in the United States sing?
"Cod Bless America."

Why did the goldfish pose for art class?
He was a scale model.

What kind of pets did the Wright Brothers have?
Flying fish.

BOY: I'd like to buy that tropical fish.
PET STORE OWNER: That fish has an expensive price tag.
BOY: Okay, but what's his net worth?

MOTHER: How could you two afford to buy a fish tank?
BROTHERS: We pooled our money.

GIRL: How could you afford to buy all those tropical fish?

BOY: I dipped into my savings account.

How did the goldfish do when he shot his first round of golf?

He had a sub-par score.

GIRL: Does your aquarium have a heater?

BOY: No. I try to keep my pets out of hot water.

My goldfish…
loves to watch pro football. He's a big fan of the Miami Dolphins.

> Knock-knock!
> *Who's there?*
> Roxanne.
> *Roxanne who?*
> Roxanne coral make great fish tank decorations.

Look at all the guppies in that aquarium. That's not a school of fish…it's an entire university.

10
Pet Smarties

What did the owl say when he saw the gate to the backyard was open?

"Who let the dogs out? Who? Who?"

What do you get if you cross a parrot with a tadpole?

A pollywog a cracker.

What is the score of the pet tennis match?

Kitty 40–Puppy Love.

How do you keep a pony and a rabbit warm at the same time?

Cover them with a horse-hare blanket.

PET ALLIGATOR OWNERS BEWARE!

A pet alligator will bite off the hand that feeds it.

A man took his alligator for so many walks, instead of alligator shoes, he bought his pet alligator sneakers.

What did Mr. Owl say to Mr. Crow?

"Caw your dog."

SILLY ANIMAL STATES

Petsylvania

Colliefornia

Mew Jersey

New Yorkshire Terrier

Mareland

North and South Dogota

Connecticat

Kenducky

Wyhoming Pigeon

Why do English cats take a break at four o'clock in the afternoon?

Because it's kit tea time.

SCIENTIST: I crossed a boa with an attack dog.
VET: What did you get?
SCIENTIST: A snake Pit Bull.

Why did the dog get a credit card?

He wanted greater purr-chase power.

What do you get if you cross a lonely dog with a crustacean?

A hermutt crab.

KURT: My smart-aleck son likes to bark like a dog
to tease me.
BERT: He sounds like the boy who cried woof to me.

How do canaries explore the ocean floor?
They use a bird bathysphere.

What do you feed a young Pekingese, the royal dog
of China?
Puppy Chow Mein.

MARTY: What do you have for homework?
ARTIE: I have to write an essay on my dog.
MARTY: How will you get him to stay still while
you write on him?

MONKEY BUSINESS

Show me a pet chimp who polishes his owner's
shoes...and I'll show you a monkey shiner.

BANKER: I'm sorry, but we won't give you a loan to
purchase a monkey.
MAN: Humph! Then I'll just go from branch to
branch until I find a bank that will.

ROB: Where are you taking your pet chimp?
BOB: He needs some exercise, so I'm taking him to
a jungle gym.

NOTICE

Rapid Monkey Groomers—tree barbers, no waiting.

What do you get if you cross a werewolf with a chimpanzee?
A creature that becomes a howler monkey when the full moon rises.

REPORTER: Mr. Congressman, do you have any pets at home?
CONGRESSMAN: I have a cat, a hamster, and a parrot.
REPORTER: Which pet is most important to you?
CONGRESSMAN: The parrot. He's the speaker of the house.

PERFECT PETS

For an athlete—a jock rabbit.

For a dress designer—a clotheshorse.

For a football player—a ram who likes to butt heads.

For an insult comedian—a mockingbird.

For a convict—a robber ducky.

Knock-knock!
Who's there?
If Fido.
If Fido who?
If Fidon't come back, send out a search party.

WHITE MOUSE: What are you drawing?
WHITE RAT: It's just a cheese doodle.

GIRL: I have a pet skunk.
BOY: Gee, that kind of pet really stinks.

Knock-knock!
Who's there?
Toucan.
Toucan who?
Toucan pet a Dachshund both at the same time.

MARY: This is my tame porcupine. Would you like to pet him?
BARRY: You've got to be kidding!

What happens when a boy goat meets a girl goat?
It's the start of a butting romance.

How did Gretel know her dog really liked her little brother?
Because her pet dog licked her Hans.

HARRY: I don't want a pet bat.
LARRY: Why not?
HARRY: Who wants a pet that just hangs around the house all day?

On my next golf vacation, I'm taking a pet rock with me to Pebble Beach.

Knock-knock!
Who's there?
I Saint Bernard.
I Saint Bernard who?
I Saint Bernard to the store to buy some dog food.

What song does an Italian cat sing?
"O Solo Meow!"

My dog...
is such a fraidy cat, he has nervous tics.

MOE: I have to get rid of Jumbo, my pet elephant.

JOE: Why?

MOE: Yesterday I taught him to roll over and he squashed the car.

KEN: I have a parrot and a dog.

LEN: Your parrot doesn't really talk, does he?

KEN: No. My dog is a ventriloquist.

What did the busy hog say when he saw the lazy potbellied pig?

"*My gosh! What a waist!*"

PET STORE OWNER: Would you like to see a snake or a lizard?

GIRL: I just can't warm up to a cold-blooded pet.

 **NOTICE**

Marco has a polo pony.

JENNY: My palomino has a golden coat.
PENNY: Wow! Talk about putting a lot of money on a horse.

STACY: Does your dog swim using the doggie paddle?
TRACY: No. He uses the bark stroke.

TIM: Is your pet llama athletic?
JIM: Absolutely. In fact, he plays baseball for the New York Yakees.

Why are cats party pets?
Because they like to go out every night.

Which dog do you find in Santa's workshop?
The Toy Poodle.

NOTORIOUS PET OUTLAWS

Al Carpone

Ma Bark Barker

Bonnie and Clydesdale

Bugs E. Seagull

The Codfather

HOW'S THE PET SHOP BUSINESS?

Bird sales are sky high.

Tropical fish sales took a nosedive.

Turtle sales are slow.

Puppy sales really bite.

Hamster sales are moving at a fast pace, but are getting nowhere.

Pet rock sales are stone cold.

What do birds do before they start to play a game?
They peck sides.

TRICKY: How are things since your parrot learned to sketch cartoons?
NICKY: Now it's "Polly-wanna-doodle all the day."

What does a three-hundred pound parrot say?
Polly want a cracker—so get moving, or else!

What should you use when you diaper a puppy?
Flea powder.

What kind of change does a horse keep in its back pockets?
Hindquarters.

What did Elvis sing to the pooch he adopted from the animal shelter?

"You ain't nothing but a pound dog."

MICK: Why did you buy a Dachshund for a pet?
VIC: That's a long story.

What did the man say when he petted the Dachshund?

"It took a long time, but I'm finally at the end of this tail."

Index